Five-Minute faces

by SNAZAROO

To find out more about Snazaroo products visit our website at
www.Snazaroo.com or telephone us on
+44 (0) 1643 707659.

KINGFISHER

KINGFISHER

First published 1991 by Kingfisher
This edition published 2012 by Kingfisher
an imprint of Macmillan Children's Books
a division of Macmillan Publishers Limited
20 New Wharf Road, London N1 9RR
Basingstoke and Oxford
Associated companies throughout the world

ISBN 978-0-7534-3463-5

9 8 7 6 5 4 3 2 1
1TR/0112/WKT/UTD(PICA)/140MA

A CIP catalogue record for this book is available from the British Library.

Printed in China

Contents

INTRODUCTION

For hundreds of years, people have painted their faces – to frighten their foes, appease their gods, amuse their audiences, and just for fun. Today, experienced face painters are in huge demand at all kinds of events, ranging from children's parties and charity functions to fêtes and carnivals.

Modern face painting materials make it possible for anyone to produce good, quick results. The water based make-up that is now available is particularly effective and easy to use. Even if you are not especially artistic, you will have great fun copying the designs in *Five Minute Faces* and, we hope, inventing new ones of your own.

Practice makes perfect

In this book we have tried to provide a variety of designs that we have found to be both popular and easy to do. Each face is clearly illustrated with a close-up photograph and accompanied by simple step-by-step instructions and, with a bit of practice, each one really is possible to do in five minutes or less!

Most people are surprised to discover just how easily water based make-up can be applied, and how quickly dramatic effects can be achieved. The simpler designs can be mastered in a matter of minutes, and as your confidence grows you will find yourself painting more and more complex designs in less and less time.

Costume accessories

Finally, the right accessories will make an enormous difference to the finished result of your face painting. So alongside the painting instructions in this book you will find simple suggestions for creating a variety of hats and other accessories, ranging from a sparkly tiara to a furry lion's mane. We hope that making them will provide you and your family with some fun as well as being a cheap alternative to the ready-made outfits that are available in the shops.

It's a good idea to start a dressing-up box, which you can fill with odd items of clothing from second-hand sales and charity shops. Keep an eye open for old felt hats, feather boas, net curtains, clothes made from silky or shiny fabric, pieces of fur fabric and trims of lace. Go to a fancy-dress shop for novelties such as party hats, false ears and noses, fake moustaches and glasses, glitter wigs, feathers and masks.

Above all, we hope that you and your models will find fun and inspiration in this book – as much as we have found in putting it together.

You will not need to buy vast amounts of expensive equipment, but the following items are more or less essential:

Water based make-up
All of the faces in this book have been painted with water based make-up. It can be bought as palettes, or as individual pots of colour. A basic palette of 12 colours should give you a reasonable start, although if you expect to do a lot of face painting you will probably find the pots more economical. A few fluorescent colours are also available.

Water based make-up can be applied quickly and easily. It dries fast and doesn't rub off. The colours can be mixed, just like ordinary water paints and, best of all, it just washes off with soap and water, even out of clothes – in short, it's very parent-friendly!

Until recently, water based paints were only available from specialist shops selling theatrical products. To some extent this is still the case although they are becoming more widely available. If you find difficulty in buying the paints, contact our mail order service listed opposite.

It's best to keep your paints and other equipment together in a handy container. A fishing tackle bag or small plastic tool box is perfect for this.

Cream make-up and sticks
Basically we recommend you avoid these. The grease make-up sticks and crayons that are sold in many toy shops and stores tend to be difficult to use and have a limited effectiveness. Fine lines are difficult to draw, and complicated designs are virtually impossible.

Cream theatrical make-up is oil based and is hard to remove. It gives a rather heavy effect and has a tendency to smudge and rub off. Also, the colours cannot be mixed, although they can sometimes be blended together on the skin.

Brushes and sponges
In order to make your face-painting technique as varied as possible, buy a selection of differently sized brushes.

It is best to buy good quality artists' brushes or special make-up brushes. We recommend that you use oxhair or sable brushes as these are both soft and firm, and easy to use.

Sable brushes are much more expensive than oxhair, but they are more versatile – you will be able to draw thick and thin lines with the same brush. Your local art shop will probably stock brushes that are a mixture of sable and

nylon, and these are also very effective.

Special face-painting or make-up sponges are the best type of sponge to use, but if you find these difficult to obtain, then try using a baby sponge cut into wedges to give you a fine edge as well as a broad surface.

Glitter

Some of the designs in this book use glitter make-up. If you are going to use glitter to decorate your faces, invest in some proper glitter gel which is designed to be used on faces. Do not try gluing or sticking on the dry glitter that can be bought in newsagents and other stores and which is intended for decorating cards and paper.

Make sure that the glitter gel does not go too close to the model's eyes. With very young children it is best avoided altogether. Glitter gel is available from shops selling theatrical products.

Extras

Ordinary make-up is not really practical for face painting, but it can be useful if you want an effect to be waterproof such as for a photograph or in a play.

Putting streaks of colour into your model's hair can add to the effectiveness of the face. The best way is to apply water based make-up with an old toothbrush or a damp sponge. Coloured hair-sprays can look good but they are difficult and messy to use and may stain the model's clothing. If you do use one make sure it is non-toxic and washes out easily.

Finally, you will need a container for water to wash out your brushes and sponges, lots of towels and paper tissues, a mirror for your model to see the final result, and plenty of moisture wipes – it's not easy to paint a dirty face!.

Download our brochure from www.snazaroo.com

BASIC TECHNIQUES

Important

Before you start face painting check that your model has no skin allergies or infections. Although professional water based make-up is non-toxic and highly tested, never paint someone's face if any kind of skin problem is suspected. If in doubt, try a little on the inside of his or her wrist and leave it for a few hours to see if a rash develops.

Preparation

Make sure that all your brushes, sponges and paints are clean, and lay them out on a fresh towel. The water used must be changed regularly.

There is no need to put any cream or moisturizer on the skin before you begin. Water based make-up is best applied directly onto clean, dry skin.

If you follow the basic guidelines given below you will be well on the way to becoming a proficient face painter.

1. First, tie a towel around your model's shoulders to protect their clothing. Keep the hair away from the face with a hairband or clips.

2. Keep the model steady by resting one hand on his or her head.

3. Always apply the base colour first, using a damp sponge. Make sure that the sponge is not too wet, or the finished result will be very streaky.

4. To achieve a deeper colour, allow the first coat to dry and then apply a second coat.

5. On designs that have a variety of light and dark colours, always apply the lighter colour first.

6. When applying colour with a brush, keep strokes even and work in continuous lines. Avoid the temptation to sketch. Confidence will come with practice.

7. Keep your designs simple but effective. Always remember that the average small child will find it difficult to sit still for more than five minutes!

8. Small children are sometimes nervous about having their faces painted. Reassure them by talking continuously, and explain exactly what you are doing at each stage.

9. Take great care when painting around the eyes. When lining the top eyelids, ask your model to keep his or her eyes closed until the paint has dried. When you are painting along the bottom eye line, ask your model to look up as you do so. Be careful not to take the paint too close to the eyes.

Note: Water based make-up is also great for body painting! Use brushes to paint rings on fingers, wristwatches and bracelets on arms, or a huge tattoo – the effects can be stunning.

To get you started, here is an example of how the tiger face on page 26 was built up step by step.

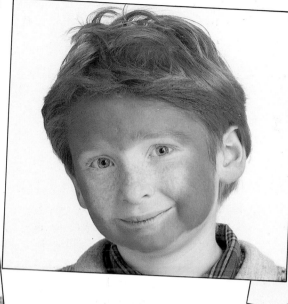

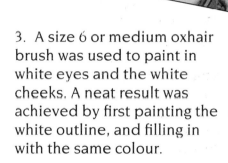

1. First, a yellow base was applied over the whole face, using a damp sponge. To avoid a streaky effect, we made sure that the sponge was not too wet.

2. A barely damp sponge was used to blend orange paint around the outside of the face, over the cheeks and up into the hair around the edge of the face. For a smooth effect, the strokes were worked from the inside to the outside of the face.

3. A size 6 or medium oxhair brush was used to paint in white eyes and the white cheeks. A neat result was achieved by first painting the white outline, and filling in with the same colour.

4. The nose was painted black, using short, upward strokes. Black was also used to paint the mouth and whiskers, and to outline the eyes. A red line was painted under the eyes, while the model kept very still and looked upwards. Finally, a fine brush was used to decorate the face with red, black and white strokes.

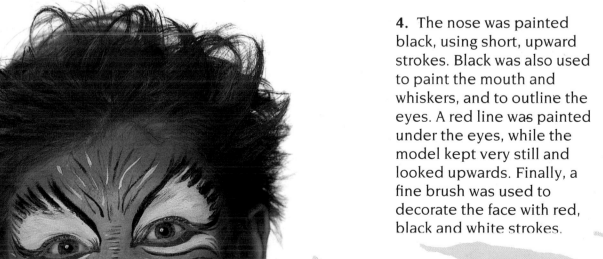

There comes a point when the keen face painter is ready to branch out beyond the family circle, and offer his or her skills to the world at large. Even if you feel that your talents are too modest for you to make a living out of face painting, you may find that they are more than good enough for fund-raising purposes.

Putting your skills to work

Unless you live in an extremely remote area, you should be able to find hordes of willing customers. Get in touch with as many schools as possible – most areas have some kind of school fête or carnival happening every weekend during the summer term. Church fêtes and local charities are a good source of events, too. Keep your eye on the local press for forthcoming events.

You could consider promoting your services with a simple leaflet – make it as attractive as possible and circulate photocopies to all likely institutions.

If you are lucky enough to live in a holiday resort, contact the holiday centres, caravan sites, amusement parks and hotels. You may be able to arrange a regular face-painting slot in their weekly events programme.

When the summer is over, there are ample face-painting opportunities at Halloween, Christmas fairs, toy shops and children's parties. In fact, the determined face painter can keep going all year round!

Running a stall

At busy events it is important to stand out from the crowd. Fancy-dress is essential – a good eye-catcher could be a clown's outfit, complete with hat and brightly coloured face. If you can persuade one or two helpers to hand out leaflets, make sandwich boards for them to wear as they circulate among the crowds. They should also, of course, be wearing colourful samples of your skills!

Sit your models on a high chair or stool, to make them visible to passers-by. Keep your face paints scrupulously clean and tidy. No one will want you to paint their child's face with dirty-looking materials!

Crowd control

Wherever you see a face painter you will see a queue of children. Crowd control skills are essential here. For everyone's sake, try to keep the queue orderly and make sure that no one pushes in.

If you can, have a row of seats and move them up one at a time, or you could issue numbered cloak-room tickets and call them out when you are ready. With a bit of luck and diplomacy, you should be able to keep even the smallest customer smiling and happy.

Workshops

Older children will enjoy trying their hand at face painting. You may like to consider setting up workshops through schools or other local centres.

When you go along to the school or centre to discuss the idea, take some photos of a few finished faces (these should be as simple and effective as possible). Also, rough out a programme for an hourly session beforehand.

1. Using a damp sponge, apply a white base.

2. Paint the pink outline above the eyes with a brush, and then fill in the area with blue paint.

3. Paint in the red nose, taking care not to paint underneath the nostrils.

4. Use a brush to outline the mouth in red, and fill in with the same colour.

5. Decorate the cheeks with yellow circles and green tears.

The photograph below right, shows an alternative design, using the same basic stages.

MAKE A CLOWN'S HAT

For a quick and easy
   clown's hat,
   you will need:
An old felt hat (try second-
   hand shops)
Some coloured felt
Glue
A pipe cleaner
A plastic flower
Thick wool

1. Cut different shapes from the felt, and glue them to the hat.

2. Sew strands of the wool under the brim of the hat for hair.

3. Attach the flower to one end of the pipe cleaner, and tuck the other end into the hat band.

MAKE A PIERROT HAT

You will need:
Some thin white card
Glue
Black paper or felt

1. Cut the shape shown below out of the white card.

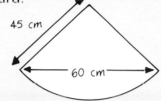

45 cm

60 cm

2. Glue the edges together to make a cone.

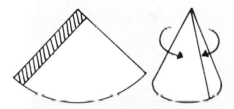

3. Cut circles from the black paper or felt, and stick to the hat.

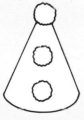

4. Make a small hole near the bottom of each side of the hat. Thread through enough elastic to fit comfortably under your model's chin, and knot in place.

1. Apply a white base with a damp sponge.

2. Blend in some pink over the cheekbones, using a barely damp sponge.

3. Use a brush to paint in silver shadows above the eyes.

4. Use a brush to paint high black eyebrows, and black triangles under the eyes.

5. Paint a thin blue mouth and add a blue teardrop on one cheek.

6. Finish by decorating with glitter gel, being very careful not to take the gel too close to the eyes.

1. Use a brush to draw the outline of the mask in pink, and fill in with the same colour.

2. Paint in the blue criss-cross lines with a thin brush.

3. Use a thin brush to paint in the white lace edging and the feather.

4. Paint the tassels at the sides of the mask.

5. Paint in pink lips.

6. Decorate with glitter gel.

MAKE A SILVER HAT

You will need:
Some thin card
Silver paint
Glue
Silver glitter

1. Cut a piece of card to measure 65 x 20 cm. Make cuts about 2 cm long along both sides, as shown.

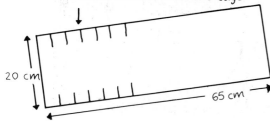

Cuts should be 2 cm apart and about 2 cm in from the edge

20 cm

65 cm

2. Cut the top and the brim from one piece of card, as shown.

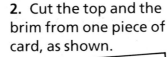
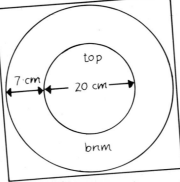

7 cm   20 cm

top

brim

Draw around a bowl or pudding basin

3. Glue the sides of the hat together. Fold the tabs down at the top, and up at the base.

4. Push the brim down over the hat, cutting the inner circle slightly larger if necessary. Glue to the tabs. Glue on the top of the hat.

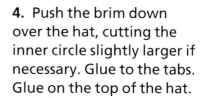
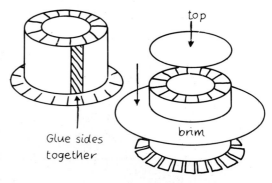

Glue sides together

top

brim

5. Paint the hat silver and leave to dry. Coat thinly with glue, and sprinkle evenly with glitter.

1. Apply a white base with a damp sponge.

2. Using a barely damp sponge, blend in some blue paint around the outside of the face.

3. Use a brush to paint silver above the eyes.

4. Use a brush to line the eyes in blue. Paint blue lips, eyebrows and the design on the cheeks.

5. Apply a little red to the sides of the eyes and to the cheek design.

SNOW QUEEN MASK

Glitter wigs like the one in the picture are difficult to make, and are best bought from a fancy-dress shop. However, to add a touch of mystery you could make this hand-held mask.

You will need:
Some thin card, about
    15 × 10 cm
Silver paint
Glue
Silver glitter
Scraps of lace or a paper
    doily
A thin stick, about
    25 cm long

1. Draw a mask shape onto the card, and cut it out. Cut holes for the eyes.

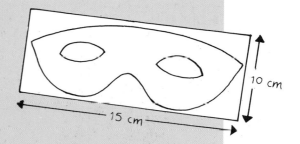

2. Paint the mask silver, and leave to dry. Cover with a thin layer of glue, and sprinkle evenly with glitter.

3. Glue scraps of lace or doily to the edges of the mask. Tape or glue the stick to one side of the mask.

I NDIAN BRAVE

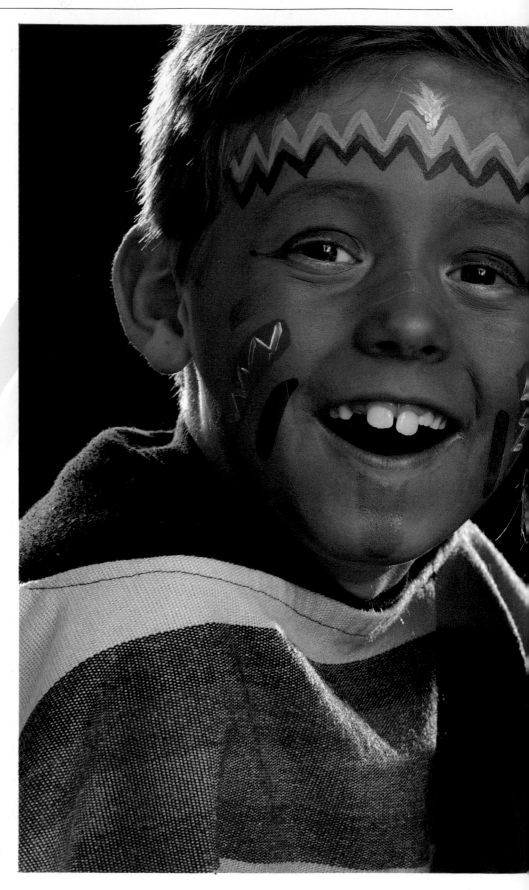

1. Apply a light brown base with a damp sponge.

2. Use a brush to outline the eyes in dark brown.

3. Paint in the blue and yellow zig-zags on the forehead.

4. Use a brush and a variety of colours to decorate the rest of the face. Copy the design shown here, or use your own ideas.

F LOWER GIRL

EASY AND QUICK!
1. Apply a thin yellow base with a damp sponge.

2. Using a brush, paint in the black lines above and below the eyes.

3. Paint in the red lips.

4. Decorate the cheeks with the designs shown in the picture.

FLOWER HEADDRESS

The Flower Girl in the picture wears silk flowers pinned to her hair. Alternatively, you could make the simple headdress shown below:

You will need:
An elasticated hairband
Coloured tissue paper
Sticky tape
A needle and thread

1. Cut the tissue paper into long strips, each about 35 x 5 cm.

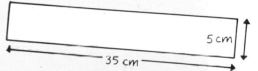

2. Roll each strip into a flower shape. Bind the base with tape.

3. Sew a cluster of flowers onto the hairband.

To make different types of flowers, cut the edges of the strips in a variety of ways.

POLICEMAN

1. Apply a white base with a damp sponge.

2. Use a brush to paint in bushy green and blue eyebrows, and blue triangles under the eyes.

3. Use a brush to paint the red nose and lips.

4. Finish by painting on black glasses and a curly beard.

Policeman's helmets like the one shown can be found in most fancy-dress shops and some toy shops.

JOKER

1. Draw a green line down the centre of the face with a brush. Use a damp sponge to colour one half in green.

2. Use a damp sponge to colour the other half of the face yellow.

3. On the green half of the face, brush gold over the lips and around the eye area.

4. Paint a wiggly green eyebrow over the other eye. Paint the other half of the lips green.

5. Outline the lips, golden eye and green eyebrow in black, using a brush.

JOKER'S STICK

You will need:
A piece of cane, about
   40 cm long
Brightly coloured ribbon
Felt
The toe from a pair of
   tights
Kapok or cotton wool
Glue
A needle and thread

1. Bind the ribbon around the cane until it is completely covered. Glue the ends in place.

2. Stuff the toe of the tights with kapok or cotton wool to make the head. Tie it to the cane with ribbon, leaving the ends loose.

3. Cut three identical triangles from the felt, and sew to the back of the stick's head. Sew a bell to the end of each triangle, and to the ribbon ends.

4. Cut a mouth, nose and eyes from the felt, and glue on to make the face.

1. Using a damp sponge, apply some red or purple above one eye to make a bruise.

2. Dab some black paint lightly over the chin with a sponge, to look like bristle.

3. Use the brush to paint a bushy black eyebrow, an eyepatch, a moustache and a scar.

4. Paint in the skull-and-crossbones in white, adding the black details later.

MAKE A PIRATE'S HAT

You will need:
A piece of thin card
White paint
Glue

1. Fold the card in half and cut out two identical hat shapes.

2. Glue the two edges together as shown.

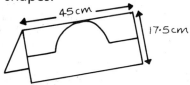

3. Paint a skull-and-crossbones in white paint on the front of the hat.

DRESSING UP AS A PIRATE

The following items make good pirate's gear:
A stripy T-shirt
Old trousers with tattered edges
An old waistcoat
A long scarf tied in a sash around the waist
A gold clip-on hoop earring
A scarf to tie around the throat
A pirate's hat or a scarf to knot around the head
Chain necklaces
A cardboard cutlass

Landscapes are great fun to paint. They are not difficult and can be really effective. Practise this beach scene first before going on to create some of your own ideas. Remember to keep your designs as bold and simple as possible.

1. Use a damp sponge to colour in the blue sea and a slightly darker sky on the top half of your model's face. Use yellow to colour in the sand on the bottom half. Wait until the background is thoroughly dry before adding the rest of the scene.

2. Paint in the red sun and the reflection on the side of the nose. Then add the black birds.

3. Finally, use a fine brush to add in the two trees. Use different shades of green on the palm leaves.

LION TIGER

LION

1. Apply a thin base of gold paint all over the face with a damp sponge.

2. Using a barely damp sponge, blend in yellow or brown around the outside of the face.

3. Using a brush, paint in a black or dark brown nose, lips and eyes.

4. Decorate the cheeks, chin and forehead with short strokes of gold, brown and yellow.

5. Hair can be combed into a wild mane, and streaked with gold paint using a sponge or an old toothbrush.

TIGER

1. Apply a yellow base over the whole face with a damp sponge.

2. Using a drier sponge, blend in some orange around the outside of the face, over the cheeks and into the hair.

3. Using a brush, paint in the white eyes and white around the mouth.

4. Paint in short strokes of black around and underneath the eyes.

5. Paint black on the nose, using short upward strokes.

6. Paint in black under the nose and over the lips.

7. Using a thin brush, paint in the black whiskers.

8. Paint a red line under the eyes to give a fierce look (ask your model to look up while you do this).

9. Decorate with more fine brush strokes around the face, using red, black and white paint.

MAKE A LION'S HOOD

You will need:
A piece of beige fur fabric, about 100 × 50 cm
Some thick, cream-coloured wool
Two ribbons
A needle and cotton

1. Fold the piece of fabric in half, and cut out two identical shapes as shown.

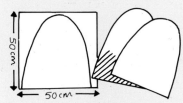

2. With the right sides facing, stitch the pieces together to make a hood.

3. Turn the hood the right way out. Slip it over your model's head, and lightly mark the face area with a pen.

4. Take off the hood. Cut a straight line up the front, from the bottom edge to the bottom of the face area. Cut out a hole for the face.

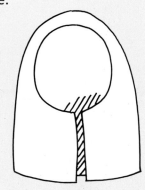

5. Sew the ribbons to the front edges, just below the face area, to fasten the hood under the chin.

6. Finally, sew on ears made from the same fabric, and add strands of the wool to make the lion's mane.

For a tiger's hood, use tiger-patterned fur fabric and omit the mane.

GREEN CAT

1. Apply a pale green base with a damp sponge.

2. Using a barely damp sponge, blend in darker green around the outside of the face and down the nose.

3. Use a thin brush to outline the eyes in dark blue. Paint the tip of the nose, the mouth and the spots above the mouth in the same colour.

4. Decorate the face with small strokes of green and blue, as shown.

PINK CAT

1. Apply a white base with a damp sponge.

2. Using a barely damp sponge, blend in pale pink over the cheeks, forehead and chin.

3. Using a brush, colour the area above the eyes in a slightly darker pink.

4. Outline the eyes in bright pink and purple, and paint in feathery eyebrows.

5. Paint the lips in bright pink.

6. Paint the tip of the nose black and add a black line under the nose.

7. Use a thin brush to outline the lips in black. Paint in the black whiskers and the black spots above the mouth.

8. Finish by decorating the forehead and cheeks as shown. For an extra sparkle, add some glitter gel.

EASY AND QUICK!

1. Apply a yellow base with a damp sponge.

2. Use a brush to outline one eye in brown, and to paint a large brown spot over the other eye. Add more spots.

3. Use a brush to paint the black nose, and the mouth. Paint black feathery strokes underneath the mouth.

Use different colours and markings to invent your own breeds of dog.

LADYBIRD

EASY AND QUICK!

1. Apply a red base with a damp sponge.

2. Use a brush to outline the face in black, and to draw a broad line down the middle of the face.

3. Use a brush to paint on the black spots.

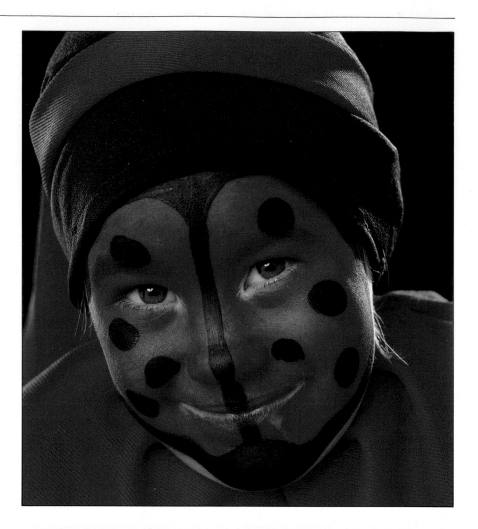

LADYBIRD HEADDRESS

You will need:
Some stiff card
Black felt
2 pipe cleaners
A black or red hairband
Sticky tape
Glue

1. Cut two circles from the card, each about 3 cm in diameter.

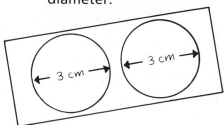

2. Fold the piece of felt in half. Trace around the card circles and cut out, to make four felt circles.

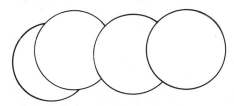

3. Glue a felt circle to each side of the card circles.

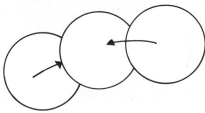

4. Tape a pipe cleaner to one side of each circle.

5. Tape the other ends of the pipe cleaners inside the hairband.

6. For maximum effect buy a red stretchy cotton ski hat from a sports shop. Put the antennae hairband on top of the hat and fold the edge over the band.

RABBIT'S EARS

For an easy-to-make
   version of the rabbit ears
   shown in the picture,
   you will need:
White fur fabric
Some pink fabric
Kapok or cotton wool
A plastic hairband
Glue
A needle and thread

1. Glue a strip of fur fabric
over the hairband, or sew
a tube to slip over it.

2. Cut two ear shapes
from the fur fabric, and
two matching shapes from
the pink material, as
shown.

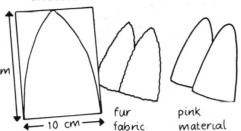

15 cm

10 cm

fur
fabric

pink
material

3. Sew each pink piece to
a fur piece, with the right
sides facing. Leave the
bottoms of the ears open.

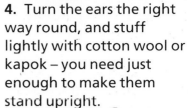

4. Turn the ears the right
way round, and stuff
lightly with cotton wool or
kapok – you need just
enough to make them
stand upright.

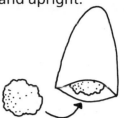

5. Sew the ears to the
fabric on the hairband,
tucking in the bottom
sides slightly.

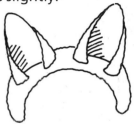

1. Apply a pink base with a
damp sponge.

2. Using a barely damp
sponge, blend in a small
amount of red over the
cheeks.

3. Using a brush, paint in the
white area around the eyes
and the teeth.

4. Paint a small red heart on
the tip of the nose with a fine
brush.

5. Paint in black eyebrows,
eyelashes and whiskers.
Outline the teeth with a fine
black line.

1. Apply a pink base with a damp sponge.

2. Using a thick brush, paint the black outline around the edge of the face, and fill in with the same colour.

3. Use a brush to paint in the white eye shapes.

4. Use a thin brush to paint the blue semi-circles above the eyes. Lightly underline the eyes in the same colour.

5. Paint in red lips and the red heart shape on the nose.

6. Use a thin brush to outline the eyes, heart shape and lips in black.

A MOUSE COSTUME

1. To make a headdress like the one shown in the photograph, simply cut out and glue a pair of paper ears to a hairband. Alternatively, the rabbit's ears on page 31 can be easily adapted using a rounder shape as shown opposite.

2. Dress the mouse in a long-sleeved T-shirt or leotard and a pair of tights or leggings of the same colour.

3. Cut a tail from a piece of cord and sew to the bottom of the tights or leggings.

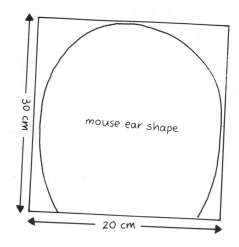

30 cm

mouse ear shape

20 cm

1. Apply a yellow base with a damp sponge.

2. Using a brush, paint black circles around the eyes, and fill in with the same colour.

3. Use a brush to paint the black outline of the lower part of the bee's wings on the cheeks. Follow the lines of the cheekbones as a guide.

4. Use a thin brush to paint in the fine black veins.

5. Paint in the black lips and the antennae above the eyes.

MAKE A PAIR OF BEE'S WINGS

A bee looks best in a stripy yellow and black jersey worn over black leggings or tights. Or you could use fabric paints to paint black bands onto a yellow T-shirt, or sew yellow stripes onto a black T-shirt.

To make a pair of wings you will need:
A piece of black card, about 70 × 20 cm
Greaseproof paper
Glue
A needle and thread
Black felt-tip pen

1. Fold the card in half and draw the wing shape shown below.

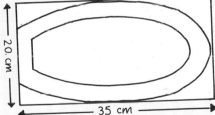

35 cm

20 cm

2. Cut out the outline of the wings and open out. Cut away the centre of each wing to leave a frame. Glue one side of the frame onto the less shiny side of the greaseproof paper.

3. Trim away the excess greaseproof paper. Turn the wings over, and draw on veins with the black felt-tip pen.

4. Sew the middle of the wings to the back of the jersey or T-shirt.

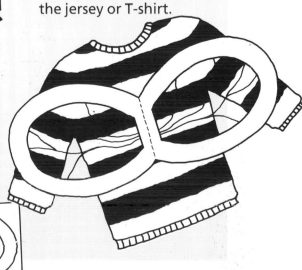

BUTTERFLY

1. Apply a thin white base with a damp sponge.

2. Using a barely damp sponge, blend in turquoise around the forehead, cheeks and chin.

3. Use a brush to paint the outline of the butterfly shape in blue, and fill in with the same colour.

4. Blend in pink and yellow around the edges of the wings, as shown.

5. Paint pink lips.

6. Decorate the butterfly shape with glitter gel.

GOSSAMER WINGS

You will need:
A piece of sheer fabric, about 60 × 40 cm
Coloured felt-tip pens
A needle and thread

1. Fold the fabric in half and draw on the shape shown below.

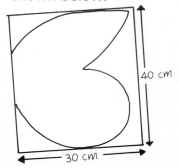

2. Cut out the wings and open up.

3. Use felt-tips to decorate the wings.

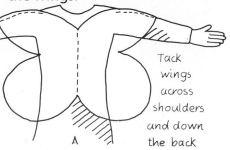

Tack wings across shoulders and down the back

4. Sew the wings to the back and arms of the model's costume – a plain leotard or swimming costume worn over a T-shirt and tights is best.

There is no end to the designs that can be painted onto a face. Here you can see hearts, clouds, birds, rainbows and sunshine. Other designs could feature flowers, balloons, kites, boats and houses.

Pick up your own ideas by looking through children's books. Or try making up designs to suit a special occasion, such as Valentine's Day, Easter or Christmas.

1. Apply the base colour, if any, using a damp sponge.

2. Use a brush or sponge to paint in the main features of the design, such as the hearts or the rainbow shown here.

3. Use a thin brush to outline the eye area, if required.

4. Use a brush to colour in the lips.

You could try painting matching designs on other parts of the body, too, such as hands, arms and ankles.

35

MAKE A MOB CAP

You will need:
A 48-cm square of material
Elastic tape
Lace edging
A needle and thread

1. Round off the corners of the material to make a circle.

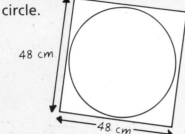

48 cm

48 cm

2. Sew the lace edging to the wrong side of the material, then press it flat on the right side.

3. Find the right length for the elastic by measuring it round your model's head – don't make it too tight.

4. Sew the elastic in a circle, about 7.5 cm in from the edge. Pin it in place to the wrong side of the fabric before sewing.

7.5 cm

VERY QUICK!

1. Using a brush, paint blue shadows above the eyes.

2. Paint in the rosy red cheeks and full red lips.

3. Use a fine brush to paint brown or black eyelashes above and below the eyes. Ask your model to keep her eyes closed until the paint has dried.

4. Finally, paint brown freckles over the nose.

1. Use a damp sponge to apply a thin white base.

2. Blend in some pink over the cheeks.

3. Use a brush to paint pink around the eyes and up over the eyebrows, and paint in pink lips.

4. Use a fine brush to paint thin black eyebrows, and to underline each eye. Ask your model to look up while you do this.

5. Paint in a black beauty spot, and add some glitter gel above the eyes.

MAKE A TIARA

For a simplified version of the tiara shown in the picture, you will need:
A strip of thin card, about 60 × 8 cm
Tin foil
Coloured paper
Glue

1. Cut the tiara shape from the card, as shown.

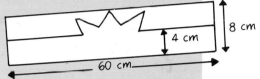

2. Cover one side of the tiara with a thin layer of glue, and press down onto the wrong side of a sheet of tin foil.

3. Trim the edges.

4. Cut jewel shapes from the coloured paper and glue to the front of the tiara.

5. Glue or staple the two ends of the tiara together, so that it fits the model's head.

QUICK AND EASY!

1. Apply a white base with a damp sponge.

2. Use a brush to paint the pink area above the eyes.

3. Paint in the red eyebrows and pink lips.

4. Underline the eyes in blue – ask your model to look up while you do this.

5. Use a fine brush and a mixture of bright colours to decorate the face with balloons and streamers, and the Happy Birthday message.

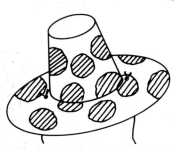

MAKE A PARTY HAT

You will need:
An empty yoghurt carton
Some white card
Glue
Poster paints
Elastic thread

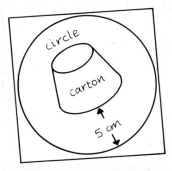

1. Draw around a saucer or bowl onto the card to make a circle – it should be wide enough to make a brim of about 5 cm when the yoghurt carton is placed in the centre.

2. Cut out the circle, and glue the yoghurt carton to the centre.

3. Paint the hat in bright colours using thick poster paints.

4. Make a small hole on each side of the brim, and thread through enough elastic to fit comfortably under your model's chin. Fasten the elastic with a knot on each side.

1. Apply a white base with a damp sponge.

2. Use a brush to paint the area above one eye in green, and the other in purple.

3. Paint one lip purple and the other lip green.

4. Use a thin brush to underline the eyes in black.

5. Use bright or fluorescent colours to paint zig-zags over the face.

6. Decorate with glitter gel, and add streaks of paint to the hair using a sponge or an old toothbrush.

MAKE A PUNK OUTFIT

You will need:
Old clothes (preferably black)
A black plastic bin liner
A belt
Safety pins

1. Rip or cut holes in the clothes and pin some of the holes together with safety pins.

2. Cut a tunic shape from the bin liner, with the closed end at the top. Don't worry about making the edges neat!

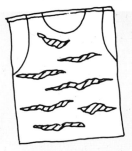

You could tear and pin the bin liner too

3. Dress the model in the torn clothing, with the tunic on top. Tie the tunic round the middle with a belt.

4. For maximum effect, use face paints to draw a tattoo on one arm; paint fingernails with black nail polish; and use gel to shape hair into peaks.

KULL

1. Apply a white base with a damp sponge.

2. Use a brush to paint the black outline around the face.

3. Paint the black area around the eyes, the nose and the mouth.

4. Paint a fine line from each corner of the mouth to the cheeks.

MONSTER

1. Use a damp sponge to apply a green base, taking the colour well over the hairline.

2. Use a brush to paint red around the eyes and over the lips.

3. Outline the eyes and the red eye areas in black, and draw in black feathery eyebrows. Outline the nostrils in black.

4. Paint in white fangs and add white dots within the red eye area.

5. Decorate the face with black lines and red dots.

A SKELETON COSTUME

strips of masking tape to look like bones

You will need:
A white or black cotton ski hat or swimming cap
Black tights or leggings
White briefs or swimming shorts
A long-sleeved black T-shirt or leotard
Masking tape

1. Tuck all the hair into the hat or swimming cap.

2. Dress the model in the black clothing, with the white briefs pulled over the top of the leggings or tights.

3. Stick strips of masking tape over the model's clothing to indicate bones, as shown here. (For a more permanent costume, use white fabric paint.)

1. Apply a white base with a damp sponge.

2. Using a barely damp sponge, shade some grey into each side of the forehead, around the eyesockets and into the hollows of the cheeks.

3. Paint the eyelids grey, using a brush.

4. Paint in black eyebrows.

5. Use a fine brush to paint a thin red line under the eyes. Ask your model to look up as you do this.

6. Paint in red lips. If you wish, paint red 'blood' trickling from the corners of the mouth.

7. Paint in white fangs.

1. Apply a red base over the face with a damp sponge.

2. Use a brush to paint around the eyes in gold.

3. Paint flames on the cheeks and forehead, using orange, yellow and gold.

4. Paint a black pointed beard, fiendish eyebrows and a black line at the outer corner of each eye.

1. Apply a white base with a damp sponge.

2. Using a barely damp sponge, blend in blue paint around the edge of the face.

3. Use a brush to outline the black mask, and fill in with the same colour.

4. Use a thin brush to paint in the black cobweb and spider, and the lips.

5. Finish by adding a white flash to the mask at the outer corner of each eye, and paint white eyes on the spider.

A COBWEB COSTUME

You will need:
Some grey or black sheer fabric
Ribbon
Fabric glue
A needle and thread
Glitter
Sequins
Tape measure

1. Measure the distance between your model's wrists when both arms are outstretched.

2. Mark the distance onto the sheer fabric and roughly cut out a circle to fit the same width.

3. Cut a hole in the centre to fit your model's neck comfortably. Cut a slit down from the neck about 20 cm long, and sew a short length of ribbon to each cut edge.

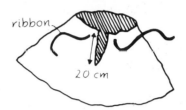

4. Lay the circle flat on the floor, and draw a web on it with the fabric glue. Sprinkle glitter over the glue before it has dried and stick on some sequins. Leave to dry.

1. Use a damp sponge to apply a green base.

2. Use a brush to outline the eyes in black, and to paint in black eyebrows and lips.

3. Paint in the black cat on the nose, the cauldron and the spider.

4. Paint the white stars and the cat's bow tie and eyes.

5. Paint the outer corners of the eyes and the flames under the cauldron in red.

MAKE A WITCH'S HAT

You will need:
Thin black card or paper
Glue
Sticky tape

1. Cut the hat brim and cone shape from the black card, and make a hole in the brim to fit your model's head.

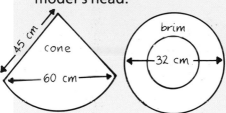

2. Make 1-cm cuts along the bottom edge of the cone.

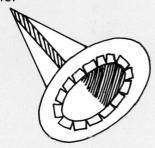

3. Curl up the cone, and fit it inside the brim. Lightly tape the cone to hold it in place. Glue the tabs at the base of the cone to the underside of the brim. Finally, firmly tape the side of the hat in place.

MAKE A CAPE

This useful cape can be made all in green (for the Monster), with a red lining (for Dracula), all in red (for the Devil) or black with a blue lining (for the Witch).

You will need:
A length of fabric
Some silky lining material
Cotton tape
A needle and thread
Cord or ribbon
A safety pin

1. Cut identical lengths from the fabric and the lining – measure the distance from the lower tip of your model's ear to the ankle for the length, and the distance around the hips for the width. Add 3 cm all around for the hem.

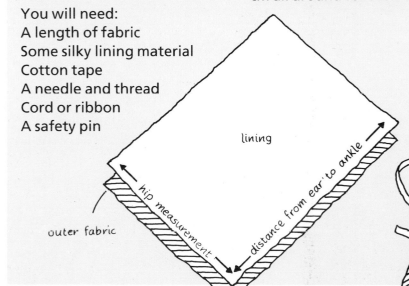

2. Lay the wrong sides of the fabric together. Hem the edges, turning the outer fabric in over the lining.

3. Sew the cotton tape across the inside of the cloak, about 10 cm from the top. Use the safety pin to thread through the cord or ribbon.

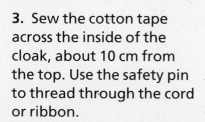

PROFESSIONAL KIT

Snazaroo has grown from its small beginning in Somerset U.K., to be the manufacturer of a worldwide leading brand of water-based face paint and children's cosmetics.

We use the same professional formula in our kits for professionals as well as our kits for children. It is a water-based formula, which means that it can be easily washed off with just soap and water. All of our products comply with European Union and F.D.A. regulations for toys and cosmetics so you can be sure that Snazaroo is amongst the safest face paints available.

GLITTER GELS

THEME PACKS
12 available

RAINBOW KIT

INDIVIDUAL POTS

18ml PALETTE

30ml

75ml

18ml

CLOWN WHITE

BOOKS IN THE SERIES

The Snazaroo website is the world's best resource for beginner to professional face painter and includes an extensive library of free photo ideas from face painting experts all over the world. It also incorporates professional face painting advice from our experts and an e-mail discussion list for the face painting industry. Also, full dates of all our face painting courses are listed. Our website address is **Snazaroo.com**.

Face painting is popular in a very wide range of activities and whether you are a playgroup, fundraiser, make-up artist, distributor or retailer you may be assured of our most attentive service.

For details of how to find Snazaroo, contact:
Snazaroo, Unit 1A-1D Brunel Way, Mart Road Industrial Estate, Minehead, Somerset TA24 5BJ UK
TEL: 01643 707659   FAX: 01643 706492   E-MAIL: Snaz659@aol.com